NATIONAL GEOGRAPHIC

Thirsty PLANET

PIONEER EDITION

By Beth Geiger and Greta Gilbert

CONTENTS

THIRSTY

BY BETH GEIGER

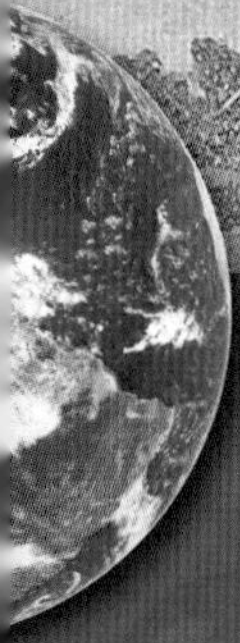

PLANET

Each day, the villagers of Marsabit, Kenya, gather at a well. They sing as they draw water from deep under the ground. With little to spare, each can fill just one large jug.

The Wonder of Water

Water covers 70 percent of Earth's surface. So why do the people of Marsabit struggle to get enough? Most is too salty. Some is ice. Only 1 percent of Earth's water is drinkable. We all share that fresh water.

Drip by drip, this water is always moving. The hot sun shines on ocean water, for example. That makes some of it **evaporate**. It rises into the sky as **vapor**, or gas.

The vapor forms clouds and **condenses**. It then falls back to Earth as rain, snow, or ice. It flows into streams and rivers and then back into the ocean.

Ice Water. *Fresh water is trapped in this iceberg.*

Quenching the Thirst

Water has been recycled like this for millions of years. The amount of water on Earth never changes. There is the same amount now as when Earth formed. Think about it. The water you drink today could be the same water dinosaurs drank long ago.

All living things "drink" water. Plant roots suck water from the ground. Leaves and stems also take in water. Then plants release water as a vapor. On a hot day, a birch tree can use up to 300 liters (80 gallons) of water!

In dry places, plants must make every drop count. A desert cactus stores water in its leaves. Some plants sleep during dry times. They burst back to life when it rains.

A Little at a Time

Some animals have special ways to **conserve**, or save, water, too. A camel can go six months without taking a sip. It also doesn't sweat. That's one way to save water!

A kangaroo rat doesn't even need to find a pool of water when it is thirsty. It rarely drinks. Instead, it gets water from the plants it eats.

Tiny Pool. *The poison arrow dart frog takes its tadpoles to pools in this plant's leaves.*

Watery Homes

Animals don't just crawl, walk, slither, or fly to water. Many live *in* it. Some, like fish, can only live in water. Most fish don't have lungs. They can't breathe air. So they can't live on land.

Other animals spend part of their life in the water. Take the poison arrow dart frog, for example. Like fish, its tadpoles don't have lungs. The mother frog carries them to a plant high in the trees.

The plant traps water between its leaves. That makes a tiny pool. It's a safe place for tadpoles to grow. Once the tadpoles grow lungs and become frogs, they leave their watery home.

Saved Water. *This desert cactus stores up water during dry times.*

Putting It to Use

You need water, too. People use it to drink, cook, and clean. An American uses about 380 liters (100 gallons) of water a day. A person in Europe uses about half that. In Marsabit, a person survives on only 19 liters (5 gallons) of water a day.

It takes water to make the things we use, too. Growing food takes the most water of all. Did you know it takes about 2,400 liters (630 gallons) to "grow" one hamburger?

Water, Water Everywhere

So many people need water. It may seem like we don't have enough. People in some places don't. Other places have too much water.

Just six countries have half of the world's fresh water. The United States is one of them. Yet people in places like Marsabit struggle. It's hard for them to get the water they need. In some places, people walk far each day to find water. Often this water is dirty. Drinking it can make people sick.

Dry Desert. *This neighborhood is in Salton City, California. It uses water from the Colorado River.*

Use Wisely. *Two sisters in Australia sweep mud from a watering trough.*

Making It Count

It takes smart ideas to solve the water problem. In some places in Africa, merry-go-rounds pump water. Kid-power brings clean water from under the ground. Some Australians reuse bath water to water plants. How can you save water? If each of us saves a little, we can all save a lot.

How many gallons does it take to . . . ?

Home

Flush a toilet? 8–26 liters (2–7 gallons)

Brush your teeth? 8 liters (2 gallons) if water runs the whole time

Factory

Make one cotton T-shirt?
2,900 liters (766 gallons)

Make one pair of blue jeans?
10,978 liters (2,900 gallons)

Farm

Grow a pound of strawberries?
125 liters (33 gallons)

Grow a pound of apples?
318 liters (84 gallons)

NOTE: Figures are for the United States

Wordwise

condense: to change to a denser form

conserve: to use without wasting

evaporate: to change into a vapor or gas; to dry up

vapor: substance in the form of a gas

WATER WAYS

***It has many names:* aqua, liquid life, blue gold. *Still, most people know it by its common name:* water.**

Picture a drop of water. Where does it come from? Where is it going? The answers might surprise you.

Earth's water is always on the move. It travels from the oceans to the sky. It falls from clouds. It flows from streams and rivers into lakes. Then it returns to the oceans.

Water's journey goes from Earth to the sky and back again. This is the water cycle. During this cycle, every drop of water is used, reused, and used again.

Just think. The water now on Earth is all the water we will ever have. There is no more. It's up to all of us to take care of it.

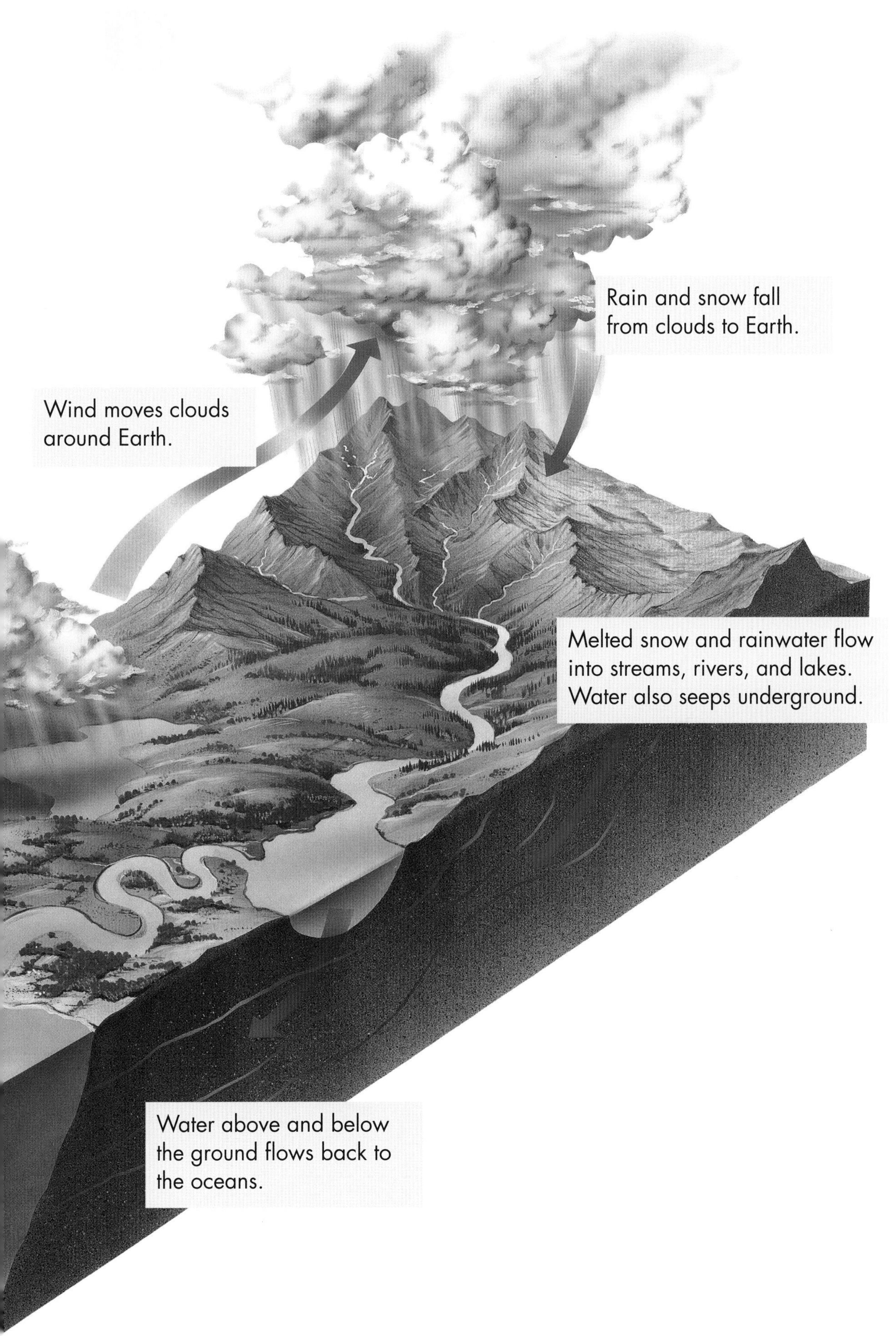
Rain and snow fall from clouds to Earth.
Wind moves clouds around Earth.
Melted snow and rainwater flow into streams, rivers, and lakes. Water also seeps underground.
Water above and below the ground flows back to the oceans.

SOME FRESH IDEAS

By Greta Gilbert

By the year 2025, nearly two billion people will live where water is scarce....

...That's almost one third of all the people on Earth today! Still, there is hope. People are finding new ways to catch water. Here are a few of their fresh ideas.

Catching Water

In many parts of the world, the water cycle is wild. In parts of India, for example, rain often floods the land. Today, people in India are trying to slow that cycle down. They catch the water in trenches. That way it can't flow away.

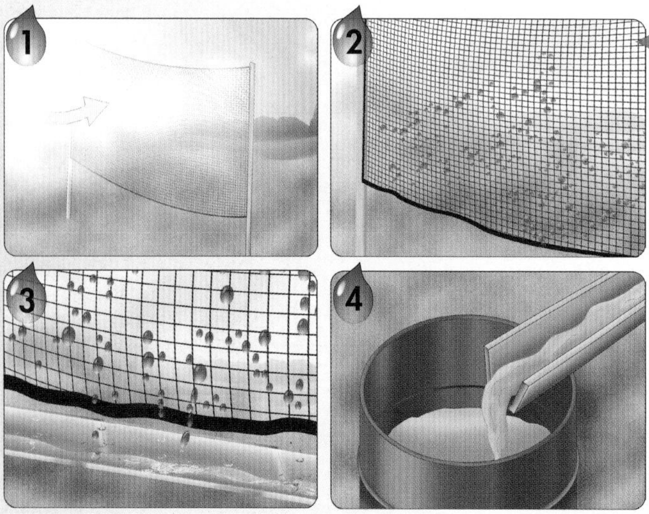

Water from the Air

Sometimes fog is so wet, it feels like you could drink it. Today, many people are doing just that. Fog-catching projects store the tiny drops of water in fog. Now that's some fantastic fog!

Water from Water

A new water treatment method can help make water safe. It's simple: Fill a plastic bottle with water and leave it in the sun for six hours. That's enough time for sunlight to kill the organisms that make water unsafe.

Water from Above

Have you ever tried to drink the rain? Then you have harvested rainwater—with your mouth! Roofs harvest rainwater, too. Gutters channel rainwater into storage tanks. That way, people can access the water at any time.

Water Wise

Let your knowledge flow! Answer these questions about water.

1. How does ocean water become rainwater?

2. What evidence does author Beth Geiger give to show that people use water in many ways?

3. Why should people take care of water?

4. Name two ways fresh water reaches the oceans.

5. What have people done to catch water in its vapor state?